THE OLYMPIC
SUMMER GAMES

THE OLYMPIC SUMMER GAMES

BY CAROLINE ARNOLD

A First Book • 1991
FRANKLIN WATTS
New York • London • Toronto • Sydney

Cover photographs courtesy of: Dave Black Photography

Photographs courtesy of: Dave Black Photography: pp. 2, 11, 17, 29, 38, 41, 42, 44, 47, 49, 51 bottom, 57; Wide World Photos: pp. 8, 14, 18, 21, 23 top, 26, 30, 36, 51 top; Sportschrome, Inc.: pp. 23 bottom (Gilbert/ IUNDT), 54; Phil Stephens Photography: p. 32.

Library of Congress Cataloging-in-Publication Data

Arnold, Caroline.
The Olympic Summer Games / by Caroline Arnold.
p.   cm. — (A First book)
Includes bibliographical references and index.
Summary: Discusses the history and organization of the Olympics, describing the individual sporting events of the summer Olympics.
ISBN 0-531-20052-3
1. Olympics—History—Juvenile literature.   [1. Olympics.]
I. Title.   II. Series.
GV721.5.A854   1991
796.48—dc20   91-4666
                                                                              CIP
                                                                              AC

CONTENTS

THE OLYMPIC
SUMMER GAMES

Women's marathon winners display their medals, Seoul, 1988.
Lisa Martin (Australia), silver; Rosa Mota (Portugal), gold;
Kathrin Doarre (East Germany), bronze.

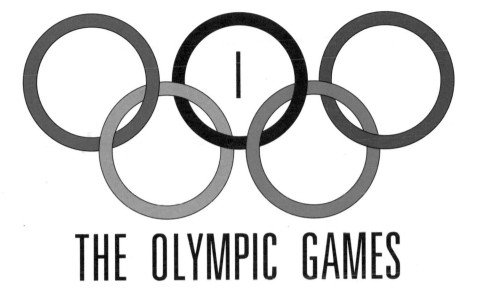

THE OLYMPIC GAMES

Every four years athletes from all over the world meet at the Olympic Games to compete against each other in more than three hundred events. The winners take home medals and diplomas and are looked upon as the best amateur athletes in the world.

THE FIRST OLYMPICS

The first Olympics were held nearly 3,000 years ago in ancient Greece. Athletes came from all over Greece to participate in running events, wrestling, boxing, and chariot races.

The five days of competition ended in a grand victory banquet with food, dancing, and singing. These ancient games were so important that even wars were stopped so that they could be held.

The memory of the ancient Olympics is kept alive with the Olympic torch. Several weeks before the modern games begin, the torch is lit in Greece from a fire on Mount Olympus and is carried to the site of the opening ceremonies. It is used to light the Olympic flame, which remains burning until the end of the closing ceremonies.

THE MODERN OLYMPICS

In 1889, a French educator named Baron Pierre de Coubertin proposed promoting athletics for young people so that people of the world would have a better understanding of one another. In June of 1894, he met with a group of people representing twelve countries and formed the International Olympic Committee (the IOC). The committee decided to institute an international sports competition similar to the games that had been held in ancient Greece. Enthusiasm was high, and it was decided that the first games would be held in Athens, Greece, in 1896. In this first modern Olympics, 285 people from 13 countries participated.

As in the ancient games, only male athletes competed in the 1896 games. A few women's events were added at the 1900 Olympic Games in Paris, and today women compete in most of the sports.

(Top) Athletes light the Olympic flame, Seoul, 1988.
(Bottom) Pageantry is a hallmark of the opening ceremonies.

Since 1896, the Olympics have been held every four years, except during the World War years of 1916, 1940, and 1944. Despite Baron de Coubertin's desire to make the Olympic Games a nonpolitical event, world politics have interfered with the games several times. In the summer of 1972, Arab terrorists raided the Olympic Village in Munich, West Germany, and later killed seventeen people at the airport. In 1976, more than one quarter of the IOC nations refused to participate in the Olympics over the issues of apartheid in South Africa and the official representation of China. In 1980, as a protest against the Soviet invasion of Afghanistan, sixty-two nations, including the United States, withdrew from the Summer Olympics in Moscow. Then, in 1984, the Soviet Union and most Eastern Bloc nations refused to come to Los Angeles, claiming inadequate security for the athletes. The 1988 Summer Olympics in Seoul, South Korea, was the first time since 1976 that athletes from most of the world's countries had a chance to compete against each other in the Olympics.

As in ancient times, every four-year Olympic period is called an Olympiad. The 1896 games were the first modern Olympiad; the Summer Olympics of 1992 will be the twenty-fifth Olympiad. These 1992 games will be held in Barcelona, Spain.

At first, the Olympic Games were held only in the summer. Many people felt that even though some winter sports had been included, there should be a separate Olympics for cold-weather sports. These Winter Olympics began in 1924 in Chamonix, France. The 1992 Winter Olympics in Albertville, France, will be the sixteenth Winter Olympics.

WHO ORGANIZES THE OLYMPICS?

The Olympic Games are organized by the eighty-nine members of the International Olympic Committee (IOC), whose headquarters is in Lausanne, Switzerland. The current president of the IOC is Juan Antonio Samaranch of Spain.

The IOC chooses the events of the Olympics. An Olympic sport must be played in at least twenty-five countries, and at least twelve countries must enter the Olympic competition. Each sport is governed by the international federation for that sport.

Each athlete must be a citizen of the country he or she represents, and every country in the world may have at least one person in each event.

The six winners of each event receive diplomas. The first three winners also get medals—gold for first, silver for second, and bronze for third. In most events, only amateur athletes may compete in the Olympics. (An amateur athlete is defined as someone who is not paid to perform.) In some sports, such as tennis, where people play professionally at a young age, the rules are adjusted. One of the greatest athletes of all time, Jim Thorpe, who won gold medals in the pentathlon and decathlon at the 1912 Olympics, had his medals taken away when it was revealed that he had been paid to play professional baseball for two seasons before competing in the Olympics. Many people objected because his Olympic accomplishments had nothing to do with baseball. Finally, in 1982, thirty years after his death, his medals were officially returned to members of his family.

Long jumper Carl Lewis (U.S.A.) leaped 28 feet 7¼ inches for
a gold medal, Seoul, 1988.

TRACK AND FIELD

Track and field events have always been among the most popular sports at the Olympics. Until 1983, when the Amateur Athletics Federation held its first world title meet, the Olympic events were also the official world championships for track and field.

TRACK EVENTS

SPRINTS

Perhaps the most exciting of all the running races are the 100-, 200-, and 400-meter dashes. In these events, contestants race flat out to be the fastest men and women on earth. Over the years, runners have clocked increasingly faster times in their desire to set new world records. Since the 1968 Olympics in Mexico City, men have been trying to break the record of 9.95 seconds in the 100-meter dash set by Jim Hines of the United States. In 1988, it appeared that Ben Johnson from Canada had done so with a gold-medal time of 9.79; however, when he tested positive for steroid drug use, his medal was taken away. It was given instead to Carl Lewis of the United States, whose time had been 9.92, and a new Olympic record. In that same year, the United States also gained a gold medal by having the winning women's 400-meter relay team.

DISTANCE RUNNING

Long-distance running is a test of speed and timing, for the runners must pace themselves to run as fast as they can to complete the race, and, at the same time, reserve enough energy for the final sprint to the finish line. One of the all-time great distance runners was Paavo Nurmi of Finland. He won a total of twelve Olympic medals from 1920 to 1932—nine golds in individual events and three golds in team events.

In the 1988 Olympics, three of the four men's long-distance events were won by runners from Kenya. Men's

Peter Rono (Kenya), gold medalist
1,500-meter race, Seoul, 1988

long-distance events are the 800-, 1500-, 5000-, and 10,000-meter races; women's long-distance events are the same as the men's.

MARATHON

The marathon, the longest race of the Olympics, commemorates the legendary feat of an ancient Greek messenger who ran from the city of Marathon to the city of Athens in 490 B.C. to report that the Greeks had won an important battle against the Persians. Today's marathon race is 26 miles, 385 yards, the same distance as between those two Greek cities. Once a year, cities such as Boston, New York, and Los Angeles sponsor marathon races in which thousands of people race, including those preparing for Olympic competition. Winners of the Olympic marathon in 1988 were Gelindo Bordin of Italy for men and Rosa Mota of Portugal for women.

HURDLES AND STEEPLECHASE

In hurdles and steeplechase races the runners must go over or through obstacles. The low hurdles are 2½ feet (.75 m) high; high hurdles are either 3 or 3½ feet (.914 or 1.1 m) high. Although runners are disqualified for knocking hurdles over deliberately, there is no penalty for knocking over a hurdle as long as the runner stays in his or her lane and does not interfere with hurdlers in other lanes. Men race

Jackie Joyner-Kersee (U.S.A.) wins the gold for the heptathlon and sets a new Olympic record for the 100-meter hurdles event, Seoul, 1988.

110- and 400-meter hurdle races; women's hurdle races are 100 and 400 meters. The 3,000-meter steeplechase race is for men only and involves jumping over hurdles, low bushes, and pools of water.

WALKING

Walking races are also just for men, and cover distances of 20 kilometers and 50 kilometers. With each step the walker must touch his heel to the ground first. To walk fast, one must swing both arms and hips in a steady rhythm. As in the marathon, tremendous stamina is needed to be an Olympic walker.

FIELD EVENTS

LONG JUMP

In the long jump, athletes take a running start, then leap from a takeoff board and soar through the air into a pit filled with sand. Because the distance jumped is measured from the board to the closest point of landing, it is important to fall forward. In 1968, at Mexico City, Bob Beamon from the United States jumped an amazing 8.9 meters (29 feet, 2½ inches), a record that has not been surpassed in twenty years. The women's record, set by Tatyana Kolpakova from the U.S.S.R. in 1980, is 7.06 meters (23 feet, 2 inches).

Olympic walkers begin the
50-kilometer race, Seoul, 1988.

TRIPLE JUMP

In the triple jump, a variation of the long jump, runners take one hop on the right foot, a skip with the left foot, and then jump into the pit. Formerly known as the hop, step, and jump, it was won in 1896 by James Connolly from the United States, who became the first modern Olympic champion. Only men compete in this event.

HIGH JUMP

Until 1968, high-jump athletes usually went over the bar with a scissors kick of the legs. Then Dick Fosbury of the United States demonstrated a new technique now known as the "Fosbury flop" in which he arched his back to go over the bar shoulders first. At the time he set a new Olympic record of 2.24 meters (7 feet, 4¼ inches), although that record has since been broken several times.

POLE VAULT

Pole vaulters use a long, flexible pole to boost themselves over the high bar. The pole vault is for men only. Bob Seagren, the gold-medal winner in 1968, was the first American to clear 17 feet, 8½ inches (about 5 meters).

SHOT PUT

The shot put event tests an athlete's ability to "put" a heavy iron ball as far as possible. The shot is so heavy that it must be pushed away from the body. The athlete stands inside a 7-foot (2.13-m) circle and spins around to gain momentum. The standard shot for men weighs 16 pounds (7.26 kg); women use a lighter 8-pound, 13-ounce (approx. 3.95-kg) shot.

(Above) Louise Ritter (U.S.A.) set an Olympic high jump record as she cleared 2.03 meters (6 ft. 8 in.), Seoul, 1988. (Right) Gold-medal-winning pole vaulter, Sergei Bubka (U.S.S.R.), Seoul, 1988.

JAVELIN

The javelin throw is a modern version of ancient spear-throwing contests. Each contestant runs for about 100 feet (30 m) and then throws the wood or metal javelin into the air. World records for the javelin throw are more than 300 feet (90 m), or about the length of an American football field. One of the world's all-time great female athletes, Mildred "Babe" Didrikson of the United States, won a gold medal for the javelin throw in the 1932 Olympics in Los Angeles. She also won a gold medal in the 80-meter hurdles and a silver medal in the high jump. She later became famous as a golfer under the name of Babe Didrikson Zaharias.

DISCUS THROW

Another event with an ancient heritage is the discus throw. Shaped something like a Frisbee, the heavier wooden discus is hurled through the air with a side-arm motion. American Al Oerter's Olympic record of 64.78 meters (212.5 feet, 6½ inches) has since been beaten several times, most recently by Jurgen Schult of East Germany in 1988. The Olympic record for women in this event was set by Evelin Jahl from East Germany in 1980 with a throw of 69.96 meters (229 feet, 6 inches).

HAMMER THROW

The only throwing event just for men is the hammer throw. The "hammer" is a 16-pound (6.8 kg) metal ball attached to a 3-foot (.9 m) wire handle. Standing within a 7-foot (2.13-m) circle, the athlete turns and swings the hammer, releasing it at the top of its arc and allowing it to fly out in front of him.

The hammer must fall within a pie-shaped wedge in front of the circle. The Olympic record hammer throw, 278 feet 2½ inches (approx. 85 m), was set by Sergei Litinov of the U.S.S.R. in 1988.

DECATHLON  HEPTATHLON

The decathlon for men and the heptathlon (the heptathlon replaced the pentathlon in 1984) for women test an athlete's overall skill. The decathlon is a group of ten track and field events that include the 100-meter (110-yard) dash, long jump, shot put, high jump, 400-meter (440-yard) run, 110-meter (120-yard) high hurdles, discus throw, pole vault, javelin throw, and 1,500-meter (1,560-yard) run. In each decathlon event it is possible to earn 1,000 points, making the overall maximum 10,000 points. Daley Thompson of Great Britain holds the current Olympic record with the 8,798 points he earned in 1984 at Los Angeles.

From 1964 to 1976, the pentathlon consisted of the 100-meter hurdles, shot put, high jump, long jump and 200-meter dash; in 1980 the 200-meter dash was replaced with the 800-meter run. As of 1984, the heptathlon has consisted of the 100-meter hurdles, high jump, shot put, long jump, javelin, the 200-meter dash on the first day, and the 800-meter dash on the second day.

Janet Evans (U.S.A.) wins the 400-meter
individual medley, Seoul, 1988.

WATER SPORTS

SWIMMING

Swimming has been part of the modern Olympic Games since 1896, when races were held in the Bay of Zea near Piraeus, Greece. Since 1908, swimming races have been held in pools. Swimming was for men only until women's competitions were added in 1912.

Individual races for men include 100- and 200-meter lengths in the backstroke, breaststroke, and butterfly; the 50-, 100-, 200-, 400-, and 1,500-meter freestyle; and the 200- and 400-meter medley. Men also compete in relay races of 400- and 800-meter freestyle and the 400-meter medley. Women's events are the same except that there is no 1,500-meter freestyle or 200-meter freestyle relay.

Many swimmers have caught the public's attention over the years. Johnny Weissmuller, who won five gold medals in 1924 and 1928, went on to a career in the movies as Tarzan. Mark Spitz of the United States holds the record for the most gold medals won at any games, with seven in 1972. Other outstanding U.S. swimmers are Matt Biondi and Janet Evans, who both won gold medals in 1988.

SYNCHRONIZED SWIMMING

Synchronized swimming, an event for women only, was added to the Olympics in 1984. Swimmers, either individually or in duets, perform dancelike patterns both on the surface and underwater to a musical accompaniment. Judges view them both from above and through windows underwater. In 1988, Carolyn Waldo of Canada won golds both as a solo swimmer and with her partner Michelle Cameron.

DIVING

Diving became part of the Olympics in 1904; today it includes springboard and platform events for both men and women. The springboard is a slightly flexible board 16 feet (4.87 m) long, 20 inches (.5 m) wide, mounted 3 meters

Greg Louganis (U.S.A.), gold medalist diver, Seoul, 1988

(9.84 feet) above the water's surface. The diving platform is a tower 10 meters (32.5 feet) above the water.

Five judges score each person's dive, rating it on elevation, execution, drop, and the smoothness of the entry into the water. Higher points are given for more difficult or complicated dives. Each diver selects his or her dives, usually starting with easier dives and moving to harder ones. The best divers use combinations of various dives, including the swan dive, jackknife, half gainer, and others. As in gymnastics, split-second timing and absolute muscular control are essential in this sport.

U.S.A. water polo player swims against the
Yugoslav defense, Seoul, 1988.

WATER POLO

In this fast-moving and rugged game for men only, two seven-member teams try to score points by throwing a ball into the goals at either end of a swimming pool. Only one hand can be used to touch and throw the ball at any time. The gold medal was won in both 1984 and 1988 by Yugoslavia.

BOAT RACES

Canoeing, or kayak races, have been medal events in the Olympics since 1936. Both men and women compete as singles, pairs, and fours in races varying from 500 meters (546.80 yards) to 1,000 meters (1,093.60 yards) in length.

In the rowing races, one, two, or four contestants sit in narrow boats called shells, or sculls, and pull their long oars across the surface of the water.

Yachting races were intended to be part of the first modern Olympics but had to be canceled because of bad weather. Over the years, many different classes of boats have been used for Olympic races. Currently there are seven yachting classes; in each class there are seven races over a set course, with the fastest times determining the winners. In addition to the yachting classes, there is also a board-sailing event.

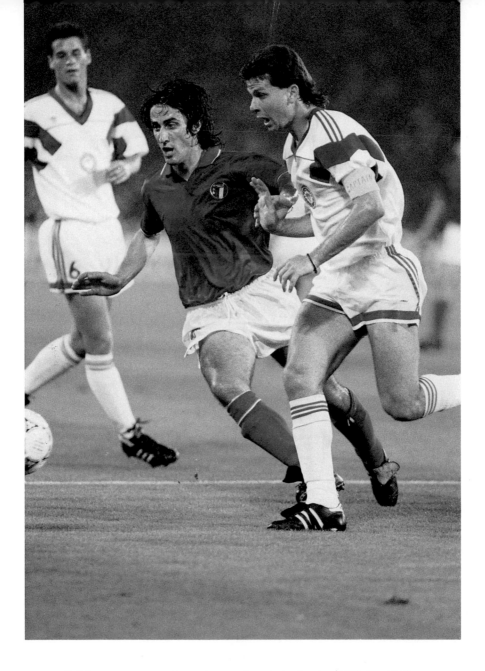

U.S.A. soccer team in action against Italy in the 1990 World Cup

TEAM SPORTS

SOCCER

Soccer, which is known throughout most of the world as football, is the most widely played sport in the world and was the first team sport played in the modern Olympics. The first tournament was held at the 1900 games. After the Federation of International Football Associations (FIFA) was formed in 1904, the Olympic soccer games came under its control.

Today, the premier soccer trophy is the World Cup, given to the winner of a tournament organized by FIFA and played in the even-numbered non-Olympic years. In most countries outside the United States, soccer players often play professionally when they are teenagers. Thus, it is difficult to form a national Olympic team of truly amateur players. Because soccer players are paid highly for World Cup play, FIFA has ruled that they can participate in the Olympics only if they did not play in the previous World Cup tournament.

The level of soccer in the United States has been steadily increasing, with the U.S. team earning a place in the 1990 World Cup tournament for the first time in forty years. In 1994, the World Cup tournament will be held in the United States. In many respects, the 1992 Olympic soccer competition will be a preview of this event. Although soccer is not a traditional spectator sport in the United States, the record-breaking attendance at the 1984 Olympic soccer games in Los Angeles indicates its growing popularity.

FIELD  HOCKEY

The strategy of field hockey is much like that of soccer. Two eleven-person teams play on a large football-sized field and try to put the ball into the goal of the opposite team. The main difference between the two games is that hockey players use large, flat sticks to hit the ball rather than kick it. In the Olympics, field hockey is played only by women. The usual uniform is a short, pleated skirt, reflecting the game's Scottish heritage.

TEAM HANDBALL

Team handball requires many of the same skills as soccer, field hockey, and basketball. Because it is an indoor sport, it is popular with soccer and field hockey players in northern Europe during the cold winter months when it is impossible to play those sports outdoors.

Each handball team is made up of seven players. The goalies defend nets at either end of the oval court, which is surrounded by walls and is similar to an ice hockey rink. The other players throw and bounce a 6-inch (15 cm) ball to each other, trying to get into position to score a goal. It is a fast-moving game requiring agility and quick reflexes. Gold medals in the 1988 Olympics were won by the men's team from the U.S.S.R. and the women's team from South Korea.

BASKETBALL

Olympic basketball began at the 1936 games in Berlin. One of the referees for the game was Avery Brundage from the United States; he later became president of the IOC. Unlike today's games, that first tournament was held outdoors. It was won by the men's team from the United States, beginning a winning streak that lasted until 1972 when the U.S. team was beaten by the U.S.S.R. in a highly controversial game. The U.S. men's team won again in 1976 and 1984, but suffered a disappointing loss to the U.S.S.R. in 1988. A

women's basketball tournament was added to the Olympics in 1976. It has been won twice by the United States and twice by the U.S.S.R.

VOLLEYBALL

Volleyball is a relatively new sport in the Olympics. Tournaments for men and women began in 1964 and have usually been dominated by teams from the U.S.S.R. Most of the players in this fast-moving sport are tall; they jump high and use their long arms to block balls or spike them over the net.

Teresa Edwards (U.S.A.) shoots a basket in a game against Czechoslovakia, Seoul, 1988.

Gold medalist Mary Lou Retton (U.S.A.) performing
floor exercises, Los Angeles, 1984

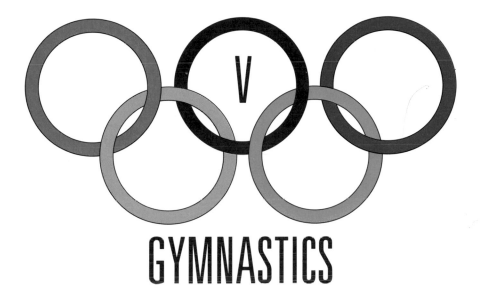

GYMNASTICS

Gymnastics has been part of the modern Olympics since 1896. In recent years, the television camera has provided spectators with close-up views of the gymnasts, helping to make this one of the most popular Olympic sports. With what looks like no effort, the gymnasts leap, twirl, and spin through the air, maintaining perfect balance and muscular control.

Gymnasts compete both as teams and as individuals. To determine the team championship, the scores of each country's five best gymnasts are added together after each event with the team having the highest total score at the end of all events winning the gold. Individuals also compete for medals both in single events and the all-around championship.

Like divers, gymnasts are judged on their technical accomplishments, with the judges awarding between one and ten points in each event. All the judges' scores are then averaged for the final score.

WOMEN'S GYMNASTICS

Women compete in five gymnastic events—the balance beam, the uneven parallel bars, floor exercises, the vaulting horse, and rhythmic gymnastics. The wooden balance beam on which the gymnast jumps, steps, balances, and does somersaults is about 4 inches (10 cm) wide and 16 feet (4.8 m) long. The uneven bars are two bars about 3 feet (.9 m) apart with one bar higher than the other. In the floor exercises, the gymnasts tumble, jump, and balance on a floor mat to a musical accompaniment. The vaulting horse is a padded bar about 3 feet (.9 m) high. Women go over the vault crosswise, whereas men go over it lengthwise.

Gymnasts from Eastern European countries have traditionally dominated the women's events, but in 1984, U.S. gymnast Mary Lou Retton took center stage with an outstanding performance in the all-around competition to win the gold medal.

Gold medalist Elena Shoushounova (U.S.S.R.)
on the balance beam, Seoul, 1988

The U.S.A. men's gymnastics team wins the
gold medal, Los Angeles, 1984.

Rhythmic gymnastics was a new event at the 1984 Olympics. In this event the women use hoops, balls, clubs, and a long satin ribbon while performing dance movements to music.

MEN'S GYMNASTICS

Gymnastic competitions for men include the vaulting horse, the side horse, parallel bars, the high bar, and hanging rings. The side horse, which is sometimes called a pommel horse, is similar to the vaulting horse except that it has two handles. The parallel bars are used for swinging and balancing. The two wooden bars are 1½ feet (.45 m) apart and about 5 feet (1.5 m) off the floor. In the high bar event the men swing and balance on a single bar set 8 feet (2.4 m) off the floor. Gymnasts grasp the hanging rings with their hands while they swing and turn, trying to keep the rings as still as possible.

Boxers exchange punches, Seoul, 1988.

VI

INDIVIDUAL SPORTS

BOXING

Boxing is another event that was enjoyed by the ancient Greeks, who wore leather straps to protect their hands. Modern boxers cover their fists with padded leather gloves. When boxing was first included in the modern Olympics in 1904, the U.S. boxers won all the medals. Many well-known professional boxers, including Cassius Clay (now Muhammad Ali), George Foreman, and Sugar Ray Leonard began their professional careers after winning Olympic medals.

Boxers are divided into groups by body weight, ranging from the light flyweights who weigh under 106 pounds

(48 kg) to the super-heavyweights who weigh more than 200.5 pounds (91 kg). Over the years, the weight limits for the different classes have varied, and new classes have sometimes been added. A boxer can fight only in his own or in a heavier weight group.

Each fight is divided into parts called rounds, each round lasting three minutes. There are usually three rounds in a fight. A boxer wins if he knocks down his opponent for ten seconds. Or, if one boxer is taking a beating, the referee can stop the fight and declare a technical knockout, or TKO. Alternatively, if there is no knockout, the referee and judges total the scores of each round to find out which boxer has accumulated the most points.

WRESTLING AND WEIGHT LIFTING

Sports of strength and defense such as boxing, wrestling, and weight lifting are for men only in the Olympics. Like boxing, events in these sports are determined by body weight because it would not be a fair test of skill to pit unequally sized contestants against each other.

Wrestling was one of the most popular sports among the ancient Greeks. Pictures of wrestlers can be seen on early Greek pottery. In the Olympic Games today, a wrestler gains points for holding, or pinning, his opponent to the ground, keeping him under his control, and for escaping holds. In freestyle wrestling, a contestant may hold with his hands, arms, or legs, and holds can be both above and below the waist. In Greco-Roman wrestling, holds below the waist, tripping, and holding with the legs are prohibited. Competitions in both freestyle and Greco-Roman wrestling are held in the Olympics.

Weight lifting is a sport that tests body strength. Each weight lifter must raise a weighted bar above his head. If he raises it first to his chest and then over his head, it is called a "clean and jerk." If the weight is lifted over the head directly, it is called a "snatch." The strongest weight lifters can lift over 500 pounds (226.5 kg)!

Aleksandr Kurlovich (U.S.S.R.) won a gold medal in
weight lifting, Seoul, 1988.

JUDO

The Japanese sport of judo has been part of the Olympics since 1972. It is a stylized form of hand-to-hand combat in which each fighter tries to throw the other to the ground or to get him or her in a choking hold.

The judo fighter wears a *gi*, which consists of loose-fitting white trousers, a jacket, and a cloth belt. The color of the belt indicates the person's proficiency, with black and brown belts worn by those who are the most advanced. Judo for women was a demonstration sport in 1988.

FENCING

Fencing is one of the original sports of the modern Olympics. Fencers compete with three types of swords—the foil, the épée, and the saber. The foil is about 32 inches (80 cm) long and has four sides. The épée is heavier than a foil, has a three-sided blade, and a maximum length of 27 inches (68 cm). Both have guarded tips. The saber is about the same length as the épée but has a flattened, slightly curved surface. It has a blunt tip but a sharp blade.

Protected by a mask and a body shield, a fencer tries to

Fencers wear protective gear, Seoul, 1988.

score points by touching an opponent with the tip of his or her sword. Modern swords also give an electronic signal when the tip is touched. Fencing moves include the lunge and parry, the riposte, and the touché. The intricate and stylized body movements of two fencers often make them appear to be partners in a ballet.

ARCHERY

Archery first appeared at the Olympics in 1900, when it was for men only. In 1904 women's contests were added and, except for a few women who had played tennis in 1900, these were the first women to compete in the modern Olympics. After 1920, archery was dropped from the Olympics until 1972. Archers compete both as individuals and as teams; they shoot in rounds, earning points for accuracy. A round of archery consists of 144 arrows, 36 each over distances of 90, 70, and 30 meters for men and 70, 60, 50, and 30 meters for women.

(Top) British archers win a bronze medal in the team competition, Seoul, 1988.
(Right) Cyclists circle the Olympic velodrome, Seoul, 1988.

SHOOTING

Pistol shooting, a favorite sport of Baron de Coubertin, was included in the first Olympics in 1896. Shooting events have varied over the years, and have included events for pistols, rifles of various types, and skeet shooting. Shooting events were for men only until three events for women were introduced in 1984.

EQUESTRIAN

Equestrian, or riding, events have been included in the modern Olympics since 1900. Men and women riders compete both as individuals and as teams in show jumping, dressage—in which riders demonstrate their skill at maneuvering their horses—and the three-day event (which actually takes four days). The oldest woman ever to compete in the Olympic Games was Lorna Johnstone from Great Britain, who placed twelfth in the 1972 dressage when she was seventy years old.

CYCLING

Except for the 1904 games, bicycle races have always been part of the modern Olympics, with riders competing both as individuals and teams. Until 1984, bicycle events were only for men. Riders race both on an indoor track called a *velo-*

drome and outdoors. The distances for the road races have varied from year to year, but recently have been about 180 km (about 112 miles) for the individual event.

TENNIS AND TABLE TENNIS

Although tennis competitions were held in the early modern Olympics, they were discontinued after 1924 and held only as a demonstration sport in 1968 and 1984. Beginning in 1988, tennis was included again but was limited to contestants under the age of twenty-one. The men's singles champion was Miloslav Mecir from Czechoslovakia. Steffi Graf from West Germany won the gold medal for women's singles.

Table tennis was included for the first time in the 1988 Olympics as well. Gold medals went to players from China and South Korea.

MODERN PENTATHLON

This event, which is for men only, tests the athletes' skill at five different sports. The event is held over a five-day period and medals are awarded to both teams and individuals, both of which were won by contestants from Hungary in 1988. In the modern pentathlon, contestants ride a horse over an 800-meter (900-yard) course, fence with an épée, shoot a pistol at a target 25 meters (82 feet) away, swim 300 meters (330 yards), and run a 4,000-meter (4,400-yard) race.

U.S.A. baseball players celebrate after winning the
demonstration tournament, Seoul, 1988.

OTHER OLYMPIC EVENTS

For the people who come to watch the Olympics in person, the host cities usually sponsor performing arts festivals with music, dance, drama, art exhibitions, and other non-sporting events. Other special events also occur, including the demonstration of non-Olympic sports.

DEMONSTRATION SPORTS

A demonstration sport is part of the Olympics, but one in which participants only win commemorative medals, not the "official" medals of the other sports. In some cases, such as with tennis, demonstration sports may later become official Olympic events. In many cases, the demonstration sport is popular in the host country. In 1956 in Melbourne, Australian Rules football was a demonstration sport. Exhibitions of Japanese archery, wrestling, and fencing were given at the Tokyo games of 1964. Baseball has been one of the most popular demonstration sports and has been played on five occasions, most recently in 1988 in Seoul, South Korea, when the tournament was won by a U.S. team.

DISCONTINUED SPORTS

In the early years of the modern Olympics, there were a number of sports that were later discontinued because not enough nations were able to participate. These included cricket, croquet, golf, lacrosse, polo, and rugby. Rugby, a game similar to American football, was played in four Olympics and was a favorite with Baron de Coubertin.

THE CLOSING CEREMONIES

When the last event of the Olympic Summer Games is over, the lighted torch is put out and the thousands of people who watched and took part in the Olympics go home. Some of the athletes will become professionals; others will continue to train for the next Olympics.

Fans cheer on cycling participants, Seoul, 1988.

It is a great honor to win a medal or a diploma at the Olympic Games as well as a reward for the many hours of training and practice. But even for the athletes who do not win, being in the Olympics is an unforgettable experience. It gives them the opportunity to compete against the best in their field. For everyone it is a chance to travel and to make friends from all over the world. Despite the problems of politics and drugs, which too often interfere with sports, Baron de Coubertin's dream of promoting understanding among the peoples of the world has been achieved.

HOST CITIES OF THE SUMMER OLYMPICS

1896	Athens, Greece
1900	Paris, France
1904	St. Louis, Missouri, United States
1906	Athens, Greece ("Interim Games")
1908	London, England
1912	Stockholm, Sweden
1920	Antwerp, Belgium
1924	Paris, France
1928	Amsterdam, Netherlands
1932	Los Angeles, California; United States

1936 Berlin, Germany

1948 London, England

1952 Helsinki, Finland

1956 Melbourne, Australia

1960 Rome, Italy

1964 Tokyo, Japan

1968 Mexico City, Mexico

1972 Munich, West Germany

1976 Montreal, Canada

1980 Moscow, U.S.S.R.

1984 Los Angeles, California; United States

1988 Seoul, South Korea

1992 Barcelona, Spain

FOR FURTHER READING

Aaseng, Nathan. *Track's Magnificent Milers.* Minneapolis: Lerner, 1981.

Fromer, Harvey. *Olympic Controversies.* New York: Franklin Watts, 1987.

Glubok, Shirley and Alfred Tamarin. *Olympic Games in Ancient Greece.* New York: Harper and Row, 1976.

Greenberg, Stan. *Olympic Games, the Records.* New York: Guinness, 1987.

Hollander, Phyllis. *100 Greatest Women in Sports.* New York: Grosset and Dunlap, 1978.

Milton, Joyce. *Greg Louganis: Diving for Gold*. New York: Random House, 1989.

Walt Disney Productions. *Goofy Presents the Olympics*. New York: Random House, 1979.

INDEX